MW01094711

The Ultimate Guide to Designing, Prototyping and Mass Manufacturing Your Product Idea

By: Jason Vander Griendt

Jan, 2017

The Ultimate Guide to Designing, Prototyping and Mass Manufacturing Your Product Idea

You have an idea for an amazing new product. You know it's going to be big, huge even. Something that will almost certainly sell itself once it hits the market. The next best thing since sliced bread!

But then you start researching. You get overwhelmed. You don't know where to start or who to turn to for advice. Will your idea even work in reality? Will someone try to steal it?

You scour the internet looking for answers to all the questions
you have, only to find there's not much out there that will help
put you on the right track (we know, we looked, it's sad).

So maybe you give up. You resign your product idea to a shelf in
your basement, never to see the light of day. Or even worse you
see someone beat you to it, produce almost exactly the same
thing the next year and go on to make thousands or millions of
dollars.

It doesn't have to be that way. We have scoured the internet looking for all the questions people wanting to create a new product ask about design, prototyping and development. Then we picked the most common and important ones and combined them with the advice we give clients on a daily basis.

The end result is what you're reading: the most in-depth guide for taking your ideas from concept to production, affordably and with the least amount of overwhelm possible out there on the internet.

Use the table of contents to jump to a section below, or read the whole thing for the full picture.

 Approximate reading time: +/- 30 minutes. Time and FUD it will save you: Plenty!

Contents

Where to Get Started (aka I have an idea for a product, now what?)

There's a big misconception when it comes to product design that taking a product idea you have and turning it into reality is something complex or difficult.

While if you try to do everything yourself that might be the case, if you don't try to learn every part of the process yourself and instead outsource to or partner with companies that are skilled in product design and development it can be surprisingly easy. By leveraging the expertise of *other* people your idea can quickly and easily be turned into a 3D design, prototyped, and manufactured, even within the same company.

Will my product be successful?

Before we get ahead of ourselves though, you may be wondering how you can know if your product will be successful. The first step to take in the development of any product is to understand your ideal customer, and do some in-depth research on your target audience. Doing this should give you a pretty solid idea of whether your product will be a flop or a hit when it reaches the market.

See if you can answer these questions:

- How old is your ideal customer?
- Where do they hang out online?
- How much do they earn per year?
- Do they have a family?
- Do they own their own home?
- What do they do in their spare time?
- Do they have discretionary income?
- What do they spend their money on?
- Do they have the purchasing power in their household, or would they have to reach for someone else's credit card (for example if your ideal customer is a teenager)?

To know if your product idea will be successful, you need to research and get a good understanding of your ideal customer.

Build up a picture of this person in your head. What problems or difficulties do they have in their lives? How will your product fix or remedy those problems? What gap will it fill that will mean they can't help but buy it?

What other impact will your product have on their life? Will it give them more esteem or prestige in the eyes of their friends? Will it make their life happier, easier, or give them more free time to do stuff they love?

Try to be realistic here rather than imaginative. You're not only in the process of validating your product idea, you're also laying the groundwork for marketing it to success later.

Answer all those questions, and you'll be well on the way to knowing if there's a need in the market for what you're planning to develop.

If you're not sure where to start, try using the Google keyword planner, or google trends to find out if people are searching for products similar to your idea online and in what quantities.

Google Trends can give you all sorts of useful info based on what people around the world are searching for over time. In the screenshot above it's easy to see

how much more popular cases for iPhones are than cases for Samsung Galaxies. This could be important to know if you were planning to develop a revolutionary phone case. Can you guess at which point in time new iPhone releases came out?

Pro tip: Market need is massively important if you plan to make a profit on your product. If there is no demand you will potentially spend a lot of time and money developing something no one wants.

It's super important to find and listen to potential brand ambassadors (whether in person, or by finding where they spend time online in forums or other hangouts. Listen to their needs, problems and what they have to say.

Not doing this is setting yourself up for failure. As a cautionary tale, read this <u>product development story about Fiat Chrysler vs. Porsche</u>. One developed a car they knew (through research) their audience wanted, and one built a car based on what they *thought* their customers would want. Can you guess who came out on top?

Doing research using Facebook's Audience Insights Tool

If you're uncertain about who your target demographic is a little-known Facebook tool can be a big help. If you know who your competitors are and they have a reasonably large Facebook fan page, head on over to <u>Facebook's Audience Insights tool</u>. Using this tool you will be able to get an understanding of your potential audience by understanding the audience of your competitors.

If you don't know any competitors, or they don't have a Facebook page that's in the Audience Insights tool, choose an area of interest instead.

Follow these steps for best results:

Choose an Audience to Start

 Everyone on Facebook

1. Choose your audience. I'd suggest "Everyone on Facebook"

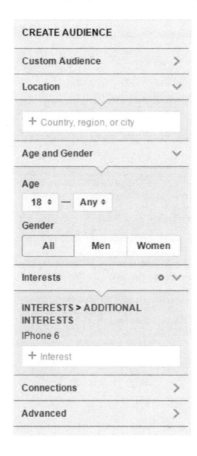

In this example I picked the iPhone 6 as an interest. You can also try to find your competitors pages as interests, although they will likely only come up if they are large and popular

2. Choose the country you would like to get results for in the left hand column. If you're unsure, remove all countries to get metrics for the whole world.
3. If you have a general idea of your potential customers age range (remember 22 year olds and above are more likely to have their own credit cards) and gender, enter these also.
4. Prepare yourself for interesting insights!
5. Start adding interests. The more you add however, the more watered down your demographic data will be. You can also add just one at a time to see how the demographics change.
6. Once you've put in an interest on the "Demographics" tab you'll be able to see:
   a. How many people are active around this topic monthly
   b. Whether your audience is predominantly male or female, and in what age bracket
   c. What sort of life they lead
   d. Whether they are in a relationship
   e. What education level they have achieved
7. Click to the "Likes" tab and see
   a. Categories your potential audience is interested in

      b.   Which Facebook pages they like, and how many people frequent those pages (how useful will this be when you come to market your product!)

You can learn so much from this one tool it might just blow your mind.

Find out who your audience is, where they spend their time, the ecommerce categories and pages they like etc. You could even go onto those pages and find out how they're being monetized to help your research on colours, designs or related products your potential audience is already proven to be buying (look for promotional status updates with lots of likes, shares and comments).

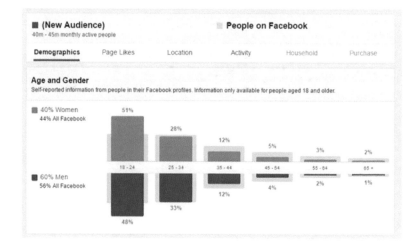

Some of the demographics you can see by looking for interests or competitors in the Facebook Audience Insights tool

Pro tip: Audience Insights is an amazing tool to learn not just about your audience demographics, but about all sorts of other things that could be important to know for developing and marketing your product.

In the Advanced settings in the left hand column you have many options to zero right in on your ideal audience, including purchasing behaviours on Facebook, relationship status, whether they are a parent (of one child, many children or expecting), their annual income or net worth, whether they

have just gone through a major life event, even what devices they own (which would be awesome for our smartphone case example!). Go crazy, there is so much info you can gain by spending a bit of time poking around and trying the different options in here.

Now it's time to look at what your potential competitors are doing.

Research your competitors well, my friend

As well as defining your target audience, it's also important to do
some market research and see what your competition is doing.
Are there any similar products on the market? How many have
been sold? 100s? 1,000s? 1,000,000s?

Try to figure out the answers to these questions:

- Why will your product be better?
- Why will customers choose your product over the
  existing product?
- How much is the similar product selling for?
- What will your product need to be priced at to make a
  reasonable profit?
- Is this figure more or less expensive than existing similar
  products?
- Why would a customer pay more for your product?
- What value does your idea add?

The more market research you can do (without letting it stop you
moving forwards with the project) the better. It's smart to know
what sales forecast you can expect as that means knowing what
profits to expect. If you expect to sell 50,000 units in the first

year, you know what the cost per part is so you will know what
the expected profits will be.

Once you've done this research, it's worth getting in touch with a
company that specialises in product development like us here at
J – CAD Inc. We can help you determine rough design,
prototyping and manufacturing costs in advance before you
spend any money on the project. Based on this information and
your research, you can then determine if the project and product
are going to be worth investing in and if they will be financially
viable.

Speaking to a company with years of product development
experience under their belt will also mean they're able to point
out hidden costs that you can be unaware of if heading into
product development waters for the first time. Hidden costs can
substantially increase production costs, so it's better to find out
sooner rather than later what the total expected project cost will
be including any potential costs you can't obviously see.

Want to work with JCAD on a project idea?

Start Your Project Today With a **FREE** Quote
We'll Get Back to You in **5 - 10 Minutes!**

Do I need to see if it's unique, that someone else has not already invented it?

What should you do if you can't find any competitors with similar products to your idea? In that instance it may be time to get a little worried..

A lot of people want to know whether a product needs to be unique, or whether it can be similar to another product. And the answer is, while it's unethical to rip off other people's ideas, if there is no precedent in the market for what you are planning on delivering, you may be setting yourself up for a huge failure.

If your idea is too unique and revolutionary, how will people know they need your product if nothing like it exists? Who will you market it too? How will you get people to understand how good it will be to own and how much it will improve their lives unless you have a huge amount of startup capital?

On rare occasions a totally new product idea can be a hit, but unless you're developing something as revolutionary as an iPod or iPhone it's hard to come up with an amazing product that no one has ever thought of before. As an aside, having the backing and fan loyalty of Apple Inc. along with their huge coffers to fund your forward thinking product – "something people don't know

they need yet" as Steve Jobs said – makes it a whole lot easier to
make, market and distribute a completely new product
successfully.

1.23 billion users is a whole lot of chicken wings..

Your product idea can be similar to what's already out there, as
long as it is substantially different. Your idea might have added
features that a current product is lacking. Think Myspace and
Facebook for example. Myspace already existed as a social
networking site and had millions of users. Facebook introduced
new features that people wanted and Myspace didn't offer.

Myspace couldn't adapt fast enough and lost millions of users. Even back in 2014 Facebook had more than 1.23 billion active users.

1.23 billion is a lot. In fact, if you were to count it in chicken wings you'd end up with 100 million pounds of them. Wouldn't you like to be the new Facebook?

Just how different your design needs to be can sometimes be a grey area. So it's better to speak to a patent attorney to double check that you are not crossing any lines with a current patent. Sadly also, many ideas are patented, and then left to rot, simply so no-one else can create them.

A patent attorney can save you lots of time, money and heartache by stopping you before you accidentally breach someone else's intellectual property rights by running with a product idea that's significantly similar to a current patent. Just doing a patent search on the internet is likely not to be enough to ensure you're in the clear.

Is this product going to make me rich?

It's the ideal lifestyle of many aspiring entrepreneurs and
product developers – relaxing on the beach while your product
sells itself and you make money while you sleep. Unfortunately
when hearing examples of people living like this, it's the outcome
which is usually seen, but not the huge efforts that were made in
the previous weeks, months or years to get to that point.

Bet you'd like to work from here. But it may not be realistic, at least not yet anyway. Image courtesy of Giorgio Montersino shared under Creative Commons SA 2.0

There's a lot of work that goes into developing and marketing a product until it is big enough to run itself, or to be bought out by another company. Passive income is largely a myth (or takes a lot of work up front), and overnight successes usually take years to materialise in actuality.

That said, to set yourself up in the best possible position for success it's important to know how to price your product.

Know how to price your product

If you've done your research in the last step, you should know
whether there is a demand in the market for your product, and
whether anyone will pay for what you are planning to create.

You should also know how much similar products are selling for.
While there are ways to increase the price of your offering and
still have people pay (think about the difference between
economy and first class on exactly the same airplane for
instance) and racing to the bottom on price is never a good
option, the price of other similar products can be used to gauge
how to price your own product. It's a fairly good indication of
what people in your market are currently willing to pay for
something similar.

Research + a calculator is your magic 8 ball for finding out how to best price your product

If no-one is willing to pay for your product, then unless you have a lot of capital behind you, there's a good chance you're going to go broke very quickly. There are exceptions where profit is not such an issue, for example in the case of non-profits and charities. Dan Fleyshman, the youngest founder of a public company has started many charity products such as giving survival kits to the homeless. He has the financial resources to do it, so why wouldn't he? But if you're just starting out you might

not have that sort of capital to throw around, and will have to
know how to price your product accurately.

Beyond looking at your competitors offerings, there are other
ways to know how to price your product, the best of which
comes down to simple math.

To work out how to best price your product:

Take into consideration design costs + prototyping costs +
manufacturing costs + shipping costs + marketing costs +
distribution costs. Add them all up, and add around 25-50% as a
safety net in case you meet with unexpected costs and need a
contingency plan. Divide this total by the number of units of the
product you're going to produce. This total is the price it will cost
you to make one unit.

Next, determine what you will be able to comfortably and
realistically sell one unit for. The difference between cost of
production and cost of sale is your profit.

If you know how much you need to live comfortably on per
month, then you can now easily figure out how many units of
your product would need to be sold each month to meet or
exceed your living costs, and to set both yourself and your
product up for success in the future.

Getting your idea ready for market

You've done your research, found your ideal audience, know
your competitors inside out, are pretty sure your product will be
a hit and will be financially viable. Right about now your product
idea should hopefully be on much more solid ground in your
mind.

Maybe you still have a few things you're unsure about though
when planning your idea's finishing touches.

Things like:

- Should my design be simple or complex?
- Should I add features I think a product should have, or
  who my target audience thinks it should have?
- Is perfection defined by me or the end user?
- Should form follow function? Is beauty or practicality
  better or are they both important?
- I'm not a designer or engineer, what's the best way to
  solve design challenges?
- I've heard of this thing called a minimum viable product.
  What is it and do I need one?

Don't worry, we've got your back.

Creating a simple product will cost less and be easier to use and understand. Your product should only be as complex as it needs to be to fulfil it's purpose. Take for instance these electrical enclosures we helped a client create. A simple product yet very effective.

In most cases a simple product will trump a complex one, especially if it involves <u>electronic components</u>. Your consumers should easily be able to figure out how to use your product, and the more complex it is the more expensive it will be to manufacture.

Because you've done your research, you should have a pretty good idea of what features your potential customers will pay for. If your research doesn't support it, even if it's something you think would be super useful to include, err on the side of caution and don't, it could cost you a lot later on. If you're still not sure what customers will want and pay extra for, depending on your budget you could:

1. rely on intuition (free)
2. conduct market research and surveys (costs involved, either money or time depending on if you do it yourself)
3. hire a company to do the research for you (expensive)

If you have the budget, you could even make different versions of your product to see which one sells the best, like the iPhone 3G & 3GS for example.

Ideally your product will be perfect both for you and your ideal user. It's important to use your market research now you've done it, and not to go back to thinking you know best, no matter how tempting it may be (if in doubt, re-read the article about Porsche and Fiat Chrysler linked to above).

Of course even in the realm of ideal products, there are some things you cannot do or that are impossible to design. This is another area where leveraging the knowledge of a design company comes in very handy, as if there are parts of your product that aren't structurally sound or are impossible to create they will explain why certain things will or won't work, and provide you with alternative suggestions.

In most cases however, almost anything is possible to create nowadays, especially with advances in 3D printing (hey, you can even 3d print replacement hip joints, houses, or full size Warhammer armour for instance..)

When it comes to form vs. beauty, typically people will choose a product that "looks nicer" over a more practically shaped product. So try to get a good balance of functionality and aesthetics. Just because a product is a rectangular shape doesn't mean it can't look good with nice rounded corners (keeping with the smartphone theme here..).

You don't need to be a designer or engineer to come up with an amazing product. If you hit design challenges along the way, the most important thing to focus on is your product's main feature. Design with this feature as the main focus, and if something additional becomes a challenge along the way you can eliminate it to keep the core focus of your product.

Also know that you can release your product in stages. This is where minimum viable products come in.

A minimum viable product (MVP) includes just the features a product needs to have to be able to go to market to check for demand. For example, a product might be fine with an ON/OFF switch to begin with, and then later the producer can offer ON/OFF/PAUSE/TIMER or other features on the same product for a higher price. These features may not be necessary to sell the product but may be desirable to some consumers.

Creating a MVP can help to reduce overwhelm, as you don't have to think of every single thing someone might want in the first iteration of your product. It's typically cheaper and quicker to design and produce due to having less features, meaning you can get your product to market sooner and start making sales. An MVP also allows you to "toe into" the process of producing and selling your product rather than jumping in the deep end and realizing it's too deep for you and you don't yet know how to swim.

Want to work with JCAD on developing a new product?

Start Your Project Today With a **FREE** Quote
We'll Get Back to You in **5 - 10 Minutes!**

How to protect your idea

So now you know how to get started on the track to making your product idea a reality and are imagining it materializing in front of you, you might be getting a bit concerned about people stealing your product idea. There are plenty of ways to avoid this from happening though, or at least to mitigate the risk (it's basically impossible to stop any product from being ripped off in China nowadays unfortunately).

To begin with, any design company you work with should be more than happy to send you a Non-Disclosure Agreement (NDA) for both parties to sign. They will most likely (or should) have signed hundreds or thousands of them by now. If you don't have one they will probably have a standard one you can use.

An NDA is basically an agreement stating the design company will not steal your idea, or share it anywhere. If they do they are putting themselves at risk of being sued and having to pay hefty damages. If you come across a company or freelancer who refuses to sign an NDA, go somewhere else.

Any product development and manufacturing company worth their salt would not even remotely consider stealing your product. Not only is it unprofessional, and could be a reputation killer – a good product development company will really care about the process of creation itself and love helping people bring new product ideas to the world.

Another way to protect your ideas are through patents. Patents are a whole other topic in themselves, and of too much detail to go into here, but there's a few things you should know.

US007864163B2

(12) **United States Patent**
Ording et al.

(10) Patent No.: **US 7,864,163 B2**
(45) Date of Patent: **Jan. 4, 2011**

(54) **PORTABLE ELECTRONIC DEVICE, METHOD, AND GRAPHICAL USER INTERFACE FOR DISPLAYING STRUCTURED ELECTRONIC DOCUMENTS**

(75) Inventors: **Bas Ording**, San Francisco, CA (US); **Scott Forstall**, Mountain View, CA (US); **Greg Christie**, San Jose, CA (US); **Stephen O. Lemay**, San Francisco, CA (US); **Imran Chaudhri**, San Francisco, CA (US); **Richard Williamson**, Los Gatos, CA (US); **Chris Blumenberg**, San Francisco, CA (US); **Marcel Van Os**, San Francisco, CA (US)

(73) Assignee: **Apple Inc.**, Cupertino, CA (US)

(*) Notice: Subject to any disclaimer, the term of this patent is extended or adjusted under 35 U.S.C. 154(b) by 688 days.

(21) Appl. No.: **11/850,013**

(22) Filed: **Sep. 4, 2007**

(65) **Prior Publication Data**

US 2008/0094368 A1 Apr. 24, 2008

Related U.S. Application Data

(60) Provisional application No. 60/937,993, filed on Jun. 29, 2007, provisional application No. 60/946,715, filed on Jun. 27, 2007, provisional application No. 60/879,469, filed on Jan. 8, 2007, provisional application No. 60/879,253, filed on Jan. 7, 2007, provisional application No. 60/824,769, filed on Sep. 6, 2006.

(51) **Int. Cl.**
G06F 3/041 (2006.01)

(52) **U.S. Cl.** 345/173; 715/234; 715/781

(58) **Field of Classification Search** 345/173–178; 178/18.01–18.09, 18.11; 715/810, 828–831, 715/234, 781, 700
See application file for complete search history.

(56) **References Cited**

U.S. PATENT DOCUMENTS

6,025,842 A 2/2000 Filetto et al 345/345
(Continued)

FOREIGN PATENT DOCUMENTS

EP 0476972 A2 3/1992
(Continued)

OTHER PUBLICATIONS

Milic-Frayling, N. et al., "Smartview: Enhanced Document Viewer for Mobile Devices," Microsoft Technical Report, Nov. 15, 2002, URL: ftp://ftp.research.microsoft.com/pub/tr/tr-2002-114.pdf, retrieved Dec. 17, 2007

(Continued)

Primary Examiner—Stephen G Sherman
(74) *Attorney, Agent, or Firm*—Morgan, Lewis & Bockius LLP

(57) **ABSTRACT**

A computer-implemented method, for use in conjunction with a portable electronic device with a touch screen display, comprises displaying at least a portion of a structured electronic document on the touch screen display, wherein the structured electronic document comprises a plurality of boxes of content, and detecting a first gesture at a location on the displayed portion of the structured electronic document. A first box in the plurality of boxes at the location of the first gesture is determined. The first box on the touch screen display is enlarged and substantially centered.

61 Claims, 29 Drawing Sheets

An example patent from Wikimedia commons

A patent is essentially a licence that gives you the sole right for a period of time to make, use or sell an invention. If someone else infringes on your patent, they can be up for a lot of money in damages paid to the patent owner (and the legal system).

While some people file for patents before having a prototype of their product idea made, it's not necessary. Patents are not super expensive, but they do cost money and you will need to engage a patent attorney to organise one. Whether or not you get a patent pre-prototype really depends on what phase you're in or how far you want to go with your idea. Maybe you only want to make a prototype to test it and see if your idea works. In that case, it may not be necessary to protect your idea yet. What if it doesn't work? If that's the case you've spent the time and money for nothing.

For more information on patents we really recommend going straight to the source and speaking to a patent attorney. The best way to find someone local is to google "patent attorney + city / state". Go and speak to them in person. You'll cut out a huge amount of the learning and research process by speaking to someone who's on top of all the legal stuff and can help you directly. If you're really struggling to find someone, let us know and we'll point you in the right direction.

But what about your product getting ripped off in China? The sad fact of the matter is that it's very hard to stop anything being ripped off overseas. To minimise the possibility it's best to use a company you trust (such as the design company that also prototyped your idea) if they have manufacturing facilities or contacts in China.

Trying to source a manufacturer on your own can be a risky business. If you plan or invest in a decent marketing strategy (more on this later) this can work in your favour as well. If your product does get ripped off, if you market and sell your product better than the counterfeiters you can more or less mitigate your risk.

From Idea to Reality (or How to get an idea out of your head)

You might be surprised to hear that you can start the process of transforming your idea into reality with a simple 5-minute sketch given to a 3D design company.

If you feel like your product idea is not yet fully formed enough for this, start by speaking to <u>someone that knows all the steps required in the product development process</u>, and who can guide you with how the process works.

Ideally this will be someone or a company that has knowledge or can work through the entire process and quickly explain what you need to know. There's the old adage that if you can't explain something quickly and simply you don't understand it, and the same holds true here.

Try to avoid your friend / uncle / cousin who has spent time tinkering on inventions in their basement or who just bought a 3d printer. There's a big difference between hobby and career inventors (although the two sometimes overlap), and you will cut out of a lot of wasted time by going to someone who works in product design and development as a living.

A summary of the product development process

*An example of a photorealistic CAD rendering where the product is placed
within its environment, in this case a spice holder on a kitchen bench*

As a quick summary, the process starts with the product design
idea and 3d product renderings. The design company can make
3D visualizations of your product that are photo-realistic and can

show what the product will look like in its environment. A kitchen appliance on a kitchen counter for example.

It's important to discuss with the design company who owns the 3D files when they're done. Some companies don't release the CAD files without further fees but a good design company will understand from the very beginning that you will want to own 100% of the design. Once your CAD files have been created, from there your idea goes into a prototyping phase, where the renderings are turned into an initial product you can hold and test for problems.

It may take a few revisions before the design is final and ready to go to manufacturing. After the prototyping phase you can get molds priced to do injection molding on a mass production scale. A good manufacturing company can walk you through all these steps, and will be able to handle all parts of the process in-house.

Costs associated with the different parts of the process vary depending on the brief, but as a general guide, the design shouldn't be too much, maybe a few hundred dollars depending on how simple the part(s) are. Creating a prototype from your designs is usually about the same or a little more than the design phase and the manufacturing will be the most expensive part of the process. If your product requires injection molding, the molds themselves will usually range from $2,000 - $5,000 for most designed parts. Price per part depends on material required and order quantity. 100 parts will be very expensive, but due to the economies of scale 100,000 units of the same part will be less than $1 each most likely.

Choosing and working with a design company in the initial stages

When you're looking for a company to contact, start by getting in touch with a design company that specializes in product designs and who ideally has worked on projects previously which are similar to your idea. It can also be beneficial to choose a design company that can do not only the 3D CAD design and renderings for you, but also 3D printing & prototyping. This will mean it's less likely for your vision to get lost in translation having to deal with an entirely new company after the design phase is complete.

The design company you work with will ideally design the parts specifically to print properly on their industrial grade 3D printers. Sadly, what often happens is individuals spend hours trying to learn 3D rendering, or pay freelancers to mock up their designs, then either try to do their 3d printed prototypes at home or with another company that has home grade 3D printers. The outcome in a majority of cases using this type of approach is that your parts won't come out correctly. For this reason it's always best to check what sort of 3D printers the design company has access to and to use their services for all parts of the process if they have the capabilities. As an added bonus it's best if the company you

work with to design and prototype can do the manufacturing for
you as well or refer you to a contact they trust to do so.

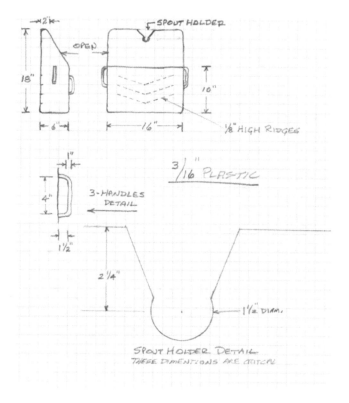

A simple sketch like this is all we need to begin the process of creating your product

To communicate your idea to a design company, usually basic sketches or pictures of similar products are all you need to provide to get a quote. If you don't know how to use basic CAD software a paper and pen is more than enough.

You don't need to be an artist to design and develop a product. Let me say that again because it's important and comes up time and again. You don't need to be an artist to design a product!

Almost every single client we have here at J – CAD Inc. is concerned that they won't be able to draw well enough to express their idea, but it has been a problem literally 0% of the time. If you can draw squares and circles that's all it takes. Just draw rough shapes, maybe a few rough dimensions and that's enough to convey your idea. Don't underestimate your sketching abilities.

Submitting any drawing is better than no drawing, and because we have worked with so many projects in the past usually we can understand your idea based on the rough drawing you submit without any problems.

The 3d product rendering made by our experts from the sketch above

This initial sketch will be enough to determine price. There is no
benefit in spending 20 hours getting all of your information
together only to find out it's going to cost you more than you can
afford to design your idea. You can spend literally 5 minutes
drawing a quick sketch and maybe getting a picture of a similar
product. After you finish the rough sketch snap a picture with
your phone and send it in for a quote. **With the right company
you can** get a quote in a few minutes. If a design company takes
days or weeks to quote, this is a red flag. They design hundreds
of parts and ideas. They should easily be able to review your

sketches and pictures and determine design cost in under an hour.

If you don't have a lot of money to start with that's okay. Getting a quote for the design should be free, so ask for this to start. You will then know how much money you need to put aside for the design and prototype to be made.

Once you have the 3D design files and prototype you can use them to attract attention and investors to pay for your manufacturing costs. At this stage before making your design public you probably want to look into getting a patent to protect your idea though.

Pro tip: When you're submitting your sketch for a quote, it's best to get a fixed price quote to design your project. Design companies offering hourly rates have no end to what they charge and your project can quickly go way off budget. If you have a fixed price then the budget always stays the same.

JCAD can help you with all parts of the
product development process, from
CAD design, to prototyping to
manufacturing!

Start Your Project Today With a **FREE** Quote
We'll Get Back to You in **5 - 10 Minutes!**

Technical validation – will what I'm planning work?

Sometimes we find people hold back because they're not sure if their product idea will be technically sound. There are probably many ideas that could be out in the world now but aren't because people feel like they don't have the technical, engineering or industrial background to know if their product will work in the real world.

The easiest thing to do here is just to ask. Speak to the design company about your idea. They should be able to guide you and tell what will and won't work. They will point out any design flaws and when creating the CAD files should be looking to eliminate any problems in the design that they see won't work.

If your product is going to have lots of moving parts, explain to the design company what you want the product to do. They will design all the necessary pieces so it functions properly. An experienced engineer / designer / machinist will also point out design flaws that will increase cost. Their job is to design in a way that will be most cost effective to manufacture. This is fundamental and one of the most important aspects of the method of design.

There's no need to worry about a (legitimate) design company telling you a product will work when it won't just to get your money. It's in their best interest to give you as much guidance as possible. A successful design project means prototyping and manufacturing. A good company won't tell you something can work when it can't as it will lead to failed projects, bad reputations and wasted time. It wouldn't make economic sense for them to do this.

If you're still unsure you can proceed with your design to the prototyping stage reasonably inexpensively. This allows you to test your design once complete with a functioning prototype without spending a lot of money making molds or in manufacturing.

Will I need to involve a standalone product designer / industrial designer / engineer in the process or should I go with a company?

Just before we get into prototyping, you might be wondering our perspective on bringing in outside freelancers to work on your project.

A 3D CAD model, 3d printed prototype, injection mold and finished silicone product – all made inhouse at JCAD – Inc

We might be biased, but typically we think it's better to work with a company rather than a freelancer. A freelancer is just a person you don't know and who doesn't necessarily have a lot of things set up that a company does such as:

- credit card processing
- refund policies
- better software
- better hardware (or access to it if it's not on site)
- more knowledge and experience
- more access to other resources
- more connections in the industry

and the list goes on.

A freelancer is also a slightly riskier proposition, as companies have often got more of a reputation on the line if they were going to do something dodgy or steal your idea.

By working with one company through the design, prototyping and manufacturing phases you develop and build on the trust and relationship you have with the company at each stage of the project. At the end of the process you have not only an awesome product, but a strong working relationship based on trust that you can leverage for any future projects.

Hiring the right company means that the whole process of design, prototyping and manufacturing can be done in-house. If instead you were to hire a number of different freelancers, too many random people involved in the same project calls for confusion, delays and a product that ends up different to what you had expected. There's a reason why they say to avoid having too many cooks in the kitchen!

By working with a company involved in all facets of the product development process, they will be uniquely placed to advise you on all the different aspects of the project, not just in one specific field which is common of freelancers. For instance, a full service company can advise you not only on CAD design, but on material selection for your project, saving you time and effort in having to research materials and processes. As another example, you might know your product should be made out of hard plastic but an expert can advise you if it should be made of ABS or poly-carbonate or something else and the benefits of each. This means that rather than you having to specify everything the company can determine the required material, or give you options if they are available so you can choose the perfect material from the available options to suit your design and budget requirements.

How find a good company or freelancer to work with

You'll know if a company will be good to work with if they ask a lot of questions about your project and express interest in your ideas. They should be very responsive and know exactly what you are looking for in regards to the functionality of the parts you are making. For example, if you need a part to be flexible they should be asking you how flexible it needs to be, so they know what material would be best to use for it.

If you do go down the route of hiring a freelancer, there are a few things you can do to make sure you don't end up getting ripped off.

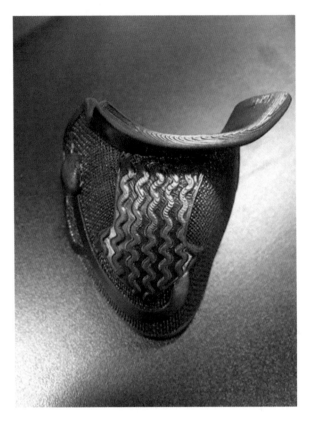

*A rubber shoe component – as an example of figuring out if a company knows
their stuff, if you're working with flexible materials the company you're talking
specs with should ask just how flexible it needs to be*

To find someone good, you can check their credentials. Ask for example work, and pictures of other products they've designed. A quick phone call can also tell you pretty clearly if they know what they're talking about. Think of it like getting new brakes on your car. If you called one mechanic and they kept saying "well, I don't know it might be $300-$1,000 but we might not be able to get the parts and I'll have to check first and find out if it's possible" then you called another and they said "yeah, that's pretty straight forward. If you stopped by today we could change them for you in about an hour for $300". You'd most likely go with mechanic #2 as they know what they're doing, are professional and sound more reputable and trustworthy.

Alarm bells should start to ring if the contractor you've hired is non-responsive or taking a very long time to show you something for review. Another red flag is if they send you work and it looks really amateurish. A design company should be able to send you a professional design to review in a few days even if it's a little rough to begin with.

Do I need to prototype my idea before manufacturing?

You would likely get a house inspection before you bought it to make sure there weren't any hidden issues. Similarly a prototype lets you check for design flaws before spending lots of money in manufacturing only to find out your design doesn't work properly. Image courtesy of Mark Moz, shared under Creative Commons License CC by 2.0

While you don't have to prototype your idea before moving to a manufacturing phase, you take a big risk if you don't.

We highly recommend that you get a prototype of your product made before moving onto manufacturing. Getting a prototype allows you to hold your product in your hands, check if your idea matches the reality you see before you, and figure out if there are flaws in your product you want to fix before moving into a mass production phase.

Not having a prototype created can literally cost you thousands of dollars in wasted product and manufacturing costs. You could equate it to buying a house for instance. Most people before making such a big investment will get a building inspection to check for any structural issues that could cost a lot to fix later on. Based on the building inspection they will decide whether or not to buy the house. A prototype functions in a similar way, by allowing you to fix design problems early in the process when your costs are much less.

As well as testing the design, having a prototype can help you attract investors that can help you fund the manufacturing phase. By having a physical part or product to show them it's easier for them to visualize and get excited about your idea!

While you're free to try and make a prototype of your idea yourself with paper, cardboard or by some other means, you won't get nearly as professional a prototype as if you get a prototyping company to make it for you.

The most cost and time effective way to make a
professional prototype

*An example of a 3d printed product. This is what your prototype can come out
like (minus the soft glow..)*

One of the most cost effective ways to prototype your idea is
with 3D printing, especially if your product will be made from
plastic (if your product will be made from metal then machining
or welding would be best). Interestingly (and maybe
counterintuitively) it's much more efficient both in time and cost
to get a company to print the prototype on your behalf rather
than trying to do it yourself. This is much the same as the 3D
design phase where it's much more time and cost efficient to

hire a company who works with CAD design day in and day out to do your designs rather than buying and trying to learn CAD software yourself.

Before 3D printing, prototyping used to be prohibitively expensive. It could cost many thousands of dollars to make test molds and do small production runs to test parts. 3D printing parts is a small fraction of this cost and is getting cheaper by the day as the technology evolves.

3D printing a simple design will usually cost less than $1,000 and can be turned around in a week or so, and no more than one month as a maximum.

Factors that can drive the cost of prototyping up

If your design requires electronic components that's where
prototyping can start to get expensive. Unfortunately we can't
(yet) print working circuits with a 3d printer. Instead they have to
be made on a one-off basis for your prototype.

Other factors that can make a prototype more expensive include:

- The size and complexity of the part.
- If machining is required or only 3D printing
- Materials required and the amount of material to make
  the part
- Any manual labour to finish the part (painting, polishing
  etc.)

Sometimes multiple phases or iterations of prototyping will be
required if the design needs tweaking after the first prototype is
made. For instance, after making changes to a design another
print of the prototype may be required to confirm the design is
final and ready to go to manufacturing.

If your product is particularly complex it may take up to 10 or
more prototypes to get your design ready for manufacturing.
Normally however the number of prototypes are kept to a bare

minimum as making a prototype many times adds unnecessary cost to the development of the product.

Pro tip: To save you money in the prototyping phase: if your product is large, a prototype can be made full size, but.. making a scaled down ½ size prototype would also be about half the cost. If a ½ size prototype would suffice then that is a great option to save money!

If you're looking for a prototyping company, your design company should know someone to refer you too, but it's in your best interest if your design company can also do the prototyping for you. Since they designed the parts they will be best placed to make the prototypes as well because they know the design intent behind the product.

If looking for a prototyping company yourself, it's best and quickest to speak directly to companies, rather than trying to get your info from non-interactive sources (we're big fans of going directly to the source if you can't tell..). To find out if they know their stuff, ask them how many prototypes they have made or how many projects they have worked on. Ask them what materials they can work with. What their turnaround time is etc.

Once the design is approved and a prototype is created, tested and you're happy the product is fit for purpose you are ready to go into mass production.

How do I go from prototype to mass production?

One of the most frequent questions we are asked about the manufacturing process (apart from price) is whether molds are required to be made for the product in question. Molds can be expensive, so the good news is that they are only made for plastic or silicone type products that need injection molding.

If a mold does need to be made, it usually takes 2-4 weeks. Once a mold is made however, thousands of parts can be made in a single day.

To determine how long you need to allow for your product to be mass produced a manufacturing company will need to know your desired quantity of parts. From there they will be able to determine an exact turnaround time. Shipping is also a factor in meeting deadlines, although typically the time needed for shipping does not add much of a delay to your order.

How to get the best return on your dollar

To get the best return for your investment, depending on the quantity of products you would like to produce you may choose to use either a small or large manufacturer. This is another area where your design company can help, either by looking after the processing in house, or referring you to manufacturers they trust and with whom they have long standing relationships. By leveraging relationships other companies have built over time you will often be able to get a much reduced price from what you would get if you tried to establish the initial relationship with a manufacturer yourself.

A smaller manufacturer will obviously manufacture smaller quantities more easily and for less money as they have less overhead. A larger manufacturer would be the opposite, however, a larger manufacturer might have better pricing on materials as they buy them in bulk. This means that overall if you need large quantities produced the cost of your parts can come down significantly. Some manufacturers have a minimum order quantity. Your best bet is to see where your order quantity lies and if you can work with the one offering the best quality samples and the best pricing.

In the same vein, to keep your costs down, it's good to have a (realistic) forecast of the number of parts / products you're likely to sell. Only order what you are confident you can sell. It's going to cost you a lot less per part to order 50,000 parts, but your price per part will go up drastically if you find yourself in the unfortunate position of having 50,000 parts that you are only able to sell 1,000 of (plus you're going to have a crammed garage or storage facility).

Pro tip: You can save a lot of money in the manufacturing process by keeping on top of trends in the industry. For instance, if too much time elapses from when you did your initial research to when the product is manufactured, technology may have changed so much that the part you are creating is some-what obsolete. For example, at the time of writing this the iPhone 7 is being released. It would not make sense to design iPhone cases for manufacture that are for iPhone 5 & 6. By the time they are designed, 3D printed & prototyped and mass produced iPhone 5s & 6s will be backup phones and hand-me-downs!

Ideally you should keep a close eye on the above during the weeks and months you are spending in transitioning from the design phase to prototype and then mass production. Keep on top of the market and it's fairly easy to avoid wasting money

manufacturing something that's become obsolete. If you don't
you might end up with thousands of parts manufactured that
you realize no one wants to buy.

Do research up front. Test. Give away free samples with an
online survey link that the users can provide you feedback
through. Gather as much information as you can to confirm and
re-confirm market need before going into mass production.

How do I find a manufacturer? Is onshore or offshore manufacturing best?

We're not going to sugar coat it. Trying to find a manufacturer if you have no prior experience in the industry is tricky, and there's a high chance you will end up with a product that doesn't meet your standards if you try to go it alone.

There are literally thousands of manufacturers all over the world, meaning it's practically impossible to filter through each one. Because of this it's best to be referred to a manufacturer by a company already dealing with manufacturers. They have already spent the time to filter through many facilities and chosen the best to work with or refer you too.

If you are going to try and find your own manufacturer, there is some due diligence you can do to tell if someone is legit and reputable. Firstly, ask questions just like you would for any other industry or service provider. This is even more important than normal as you will likely be spending a substantial amount of money with them. Ask them for samples. Do what you need to do to make you feel confident to work with them. If there's anything that doesn't feel right, go with your gut and find someone else.

Plastic injection molds at one of our manufacturing facilities

If looking for a manufacturer you will need to decide whether you want to work with someone in America or Canada, or whether to outsource to a country like China. The difference between the two is mainly cost-based.

Working in the US can cost 20 – 80% + more than working in an Eastern country. Some argue that quality is better in the US, and in some instances perhaps this is correct. What is important to understand though is that China and other Asian countries have been manufacturing the world's products now for more than 20 years. They are experts and their quality is on par if not better than US manufacturing in regards to efficiency, speed and price. Most of your car parts, household goods and clothing is made in China, and there is a reason that is the case.

If you are going to try and find a manufacturer yourself, you can search for one on Alibaba.com or similar sites but how do you choose the best supplier in Asia from among thousands without making a company killing mistake?

Definitely don't go for the lowest cost vendor possible as you're likely to be disappointed. Choose the best, in regards to price, turnaround time and quality. Choosing only based on price will not get you the best product manufacturing supplier.

Quality and reputation are both very important. The higher the reputation the higher the price will most likely be. A company that is not known and has no references is a riskier one to work with. If you are willing to spend the time to do your due diligence intelligently (even to the point of visiting the facility in person if you're looking at spending a large amount of money) you can find quality companies at a quality price – remember that every company started out without references at some point. You can also ask other companies in the industry for advice. You might be surprised how willing they are and what lengths they'll go to in order to help you for free.

If you're just starting out though, you'll save yourself a lot of headaches (and potentially heartache) by sticking with the design and prototyping company or having them refer you to a manufacturer. If they have their own manufacturing facility then you have nothing to worry about. They will take care of it all for you. This is the number one way to go. Referrals are your next best choice.

By referring you to a manufacturer, a company is putting their reputation on the line by giving the referral, which usually means they will only send you on to a trusted source. Unless your original designer or supplier is unscrupulous and only working with you to make as much money as possible without care for the end-product churn-and-burn style you should be fine.

Finding your own manufacturer should be your last choice as it will be the most uncertain, and the most time consuming. In some ways though it's no different than looking for a builder local to you. You wouldn't walk into a builder's showroom, pick a plan from a picture and get them to start building tomorrow. You'd ask friends and family for a referral and find out as much about the builder as you could. This is even more important when spending thousands of dollars in a different country, with a 12 hour time difference, and being unsure about how your end product will turn out or uncertain whether you'll be served properly or ripped off.

Once you've designed and prototyped your product with us we can also manufacture it inhouse, whether you just want 500 pieces or you need 500,000

Start Your Project Today With a **FREE** Quote
We'll Get Back to You in **5 - 10 Minutes!**

Last bits and pieces to think about (aka product packaging and marketing)

Hopefully by this point you're getting excited and are already imagining your product on the shelves of major stores around the world. But there are still a few loose ends to wrap up. Even if you have the world's best product if you have no marketing campaign or strategy prepared for it, it probably isn't going to do so well. Even if it will spread like wild fire through word-of-mouth, the first buyers (or people you give free samples to, to help spread the word) still need to find their way to it somehow.

Part of a strong marketing campaign is an iconic logo, memorable packaging and a strong brand. Look at how DollarShaveClub brand themselves and package their products for instance.

Pro tip: A logo and packaging don't need to be expensive. The manufacturer can usually arrange packaging as well, even to the point of designing it in house for free or a minimal charge seeing as you will be spending so much money with them otherwise.

When should you factor in packaging?

You don't completely need to worry about packaging and branding until your product is ready (it can be a time waster at the beginning when you have nothing to package), but it should be factored into the end cost of each unit. The price for packaging will change depending on the type of packaging you need, eg. Is it cardboard? Plastic? Printed? Shrink wrap? Price for packaging will also depend on the size of your product. But when it comes down to it, you're not looking at that much, with packaging potentially adding a few cents or a few dollars per part.

If the company you're working with is unwilling to do your design work or is outside your budget for logos and packaging, in a world of freelance marketplaces, it's not too hard to find a good designer. Depending on your budget you could look to fiverr (but don't spend $5, find a designer you like, and buy their premium packages, they will cost a little more, but it's very hard to get something you like first time for $5).

Fiverr pro tip: If you're looking on fiverr for an artist, look for people who have completed lots of jobs and have perfect reviews. But also look for consistency in their portfolios. Usually people will show their best work up the front of their

portfolio. If the quality of work gets progressively worse as you go through the portfolio, look at someone else. Also make sure the style is consistent. Work styles that aren't consistent can indicate that the work in their portfolio is not their own.

Other options for finding good designers at a reasonable price are to use a crowdsourced design platform like 99designs or looking through the portfolios of designers for hire on dribble. Look specifically for people who have designed logos and product packaging in the style you're looking for.

As a back up, consider posting a job on websites like Upwork, Freelancer or other freelancing marketplaces.

Freelancing website pro tip: You will likely get a lot of spammy job bids (a lot.. and if you put your phone number in the job people will harass you over the phone too..) from people who haven't even read your ad properly. To cover yourself for this in advance, put a question into the job description people need to answer (Something like "what's the twelfth letter in the alphabet" or "what is the square root of 9", something a little challenging but not cryptic) and ignore all responses who don't answer your question. Another dead giveaway that the job bid is generic is if it's addressed to "Dear sir or madam" or something similar rather than addressing you by your name. On

some platforms you can constrain the countries from which people can respond to your job. Unless you really know what to look for and what to avoid, you will have better results and less frustration hiring from the United States, Australia, Canada and the United Kingdom, but you will need to pay more.

What about marketing?

When it comes to marketing your product we have almost gone full circle, and now's a good time to look back to the market research you did in the initial phases of planning your product development. There are many different ways to market a product but the type of product you are creating, and where you know the audience for it spends time will be your best indicators when developing a marketing strategy.

Knowing how much profit you get from every dollar you spend on marketing is the closest you'll ever come to printing your own money. Image courtesy of TaxCredits.net shared under Creative Commons license CC by 2.0

Pay per click advertising

If people will be searching for your product online then an online marketing campaign would be most ideal, most likely one involving pay per click (PPC) campaigns, such as using Google Adwords, paid Twitter Ads, sponsored influencer marketing etc. Clicks can be expensive but PPC is generally a good way to start as you control your spend, you start getting feedback on your product / website / landing page immediately, and can target your ads specifically to the interests or searches of your ideal customer. You can also track conversions specific to ad spend, so you know how much it costs in to sell one unit of your product. If you can spend less on ads to acquire a customer than it costs to produce your product you are onto a winner. This is the closest you'll ever come to printing your own money, as you know how much profit you can get back for every dollar you spend on ads and can scale your campaigns exponentially.

Search Engine Optimization

Search Engine Optimization (SEO) to get organic search engine traffic is ideal if you are already established, and have a budget that you can invest into an ongoing campaign without seeing much of a return over the first couple of months. Typically if no SEO work has been done previously it can take 2 – 6 months to see a return on your marketing investment.

Where PPC advertising on platforms outside of Google is interruption marketing (eg. someone is on facebook looking at funny cat videos, and your ad has to be good enough to interrupt their train of thought and get them to take action), when people are searching for a product online, they are often ready to buy and just looking for the best product or retailer to meet their needs.

If someone has an adblocker or ad blindness (where they skip past or ignore ads on a page) then adwords can become ineffective, and so conversions can be higher for organic website traffic obtained through search engine optimization than through advertising for the same cost. If you have the budget a combination of PPC advertising and SEO can also be a good way to go, as you can start getting traffic immediately, but over the long term can also build up your organic visitors.

Traditional advertising

There is a saying in the advertising world that 50% of your advertising budget is wasted, you just don't know which 50%. With more modern forms of advertising where statistics, ad spend and conversions can be tracked this is not so applicable, however it remains very true in more traditional forms of advertising, such as using radio or television ads, or putting ads on bus stops or in newspapers or magazines.

*Even if thousands of people see this bus stop ad it won't matter if they're all
Toyota, Nissan and Mazda drivers. Image courtesy of Anup K.D. Sayare*

The draw back of these methods is that the advertising is much
less direct, and you are hoping to get in front of your ideal
audience, but in reality are likely to be reaching many people
who will not be interested. And it's very difficult to know exactly
where your marketing is effective.

Doing your own marketing

If you want to do your own marketing, especially online, there
are many different guides or training courses you can follow
depending on the method you decide to use. Things change very
quickly however in online marketing, so make sure the
information you are consuming and using is up to date or you
can do more harm than good.

If you can afford it, it's best to bring on a professional marketing
agency with a solid reputation in bringing in new customers to
manage your marketing campaigns and strategies.

The other way to go is to try and get your product into stores
directly, in order to leverage other people's marketing efforts.

If you like the sound of this approach, it's best if you can directly
approach local store owners, get to know them, and then
convince them (in the nicest possible way) to sell your product in
their store. Once your product is in a few stores, from there you
can see how it sells. If it sells well, you can approach other
retailers with the sales results you have already achieved as
incentive for them to stock your product too.

If your product is for the mass consumer then you'll need to get in contact with massive distributors and get them to place an equally massive order. While this is not impossible it is much easier to start small and work your way to larger things. Starting small will allow you to get publicity which will snowball if your product is successful.

At this point other larger retailers will start to approach you, allowing you to name your price. If you approach large retailers before the product is proven however you might end up signing contracts that are not in your best interests and that give your product away at a fraction of the profit you could have otherwise made.

That's it, go take action and make your product idea a reality!

If you need some inspiration, an excellent movie to watch all about the struggle of going from idea to manufacturing is Joy. Go watch the trailer (or movie), get inspired and then start taking action on making your product dream a reality!

If you're still reading, you're well on your way now to getting your first (or next) product to market.

Don't get stuck in analysis paralysis. You now know everything you need to in order to begin the journey of getting your idea out to the world. So what are you waiting for?

One of the most common characteristics of successful entrepreneurs is their ability to take rapid action, and to quickly move forwards with turning their ideas into reality.

If you really still feel stuck, then feel free to get in touch directly, either on email or by calling 1-888-202-2052. I love talking about this stuff and helping people realize their product dreams, and am happy to work through any ideas you might have. Similarly if you need a company you can trust, give me a call or send through a quote request, and let's start working together!

Otherwise, feel free to leave feedback or questions in the comments below, I'll answer them all, there's no silly questions.

And if you found this guide useful please help it spread by sharing it on your social media profiles, or forwarding it to anyone you know would be interested.

Thanks for reading!

About Jason

Jason Vander Griendt went to school for mechanical engineering design. He spent many years working in manufacturing environments as well as being employed by some of the largest engineering companies in the world. He has almost 20 years experience in the areas of manufacturing and engineering and has owned J – CAD Inc. since 2006.

J – CAD Inc. are 3D experts, offering expert product design and engineering as well as 3D printing in many different materials and prototyping. Once the prototyping phase is complete J – CAD Inc. can manufacture your parts on a mass production scale at their facility in Shenzhen, China and ship your parts globally.

J – CAD Inc. have worked with clients all around the world, including in their home town of Toronto, Canada although 90% of their clients are located in virtually every major city and state in the USA including New York City, Los Angeles, Chicago, Houston, Philadelphia, Phoenix, San Antonio, San Diego, Dallas, San Jose, Austin, Jacksonville, San Francisco, Indianapolis, Columbus, Fort Worth, Charlotte, Detroit, El Paso, Seattle, Denver, Washington DC, Memphis, Boston, Nashville, Baltimore, Oklahoma City, Portland, Las Vegas, Louisville, Milwaukee, Albuquerque, Tucson, Fresno, Sacramento, Long Beach, Kansas

City, Mesa, Atlanta, Virginia Beach, Omaha, Colorado Springs, Raleigh, Miami, Oakland, Minneapolis, Tulsa, Cleveland, Wichita, New Orleans, Arlington, Worcester and more! We have also worked with clients in Australia, New Zealand, Morocco, Tunisia, Greece, Italy, Spain, France, Portugal, Germany, Netherlands, Austria, Ireland, United Kingdom, Scotland, Denmark, Norway, Sweden, Finland, Ukraine, Romania, Poland, China, Thailand, India, Russia, Bulgaria, Belarus, Hungary, Czech Republic, Slovakia, Slovenia, Belgium, Macedonia, Albania, Moldova, Switzerland, Serbia, Egypt, Armenia, Turkey, Croatia and the list is still growing!

Following is a small selection of renderings, products and parts JCAD – Inc has created on behalf of their clients

Got an idea you need help with?

Start Your Project Today With a **FREE** Quote
We'll Get Back to You in **5 - 10 Minutes!**

jcadinternational

As seen on

Contact Jason through http://jcadusa.com/contact/, on 1-888-202-2052 or at info@jcadusa.com for a free quote on your next product idea, for media requests, or if you just want to talk shop

Questions?

Call J – CAD Inc. directly to discuss your project with one of our experts 1.888.202.2052 or email info@jcadusa.com

Visit us: www.jcadusa.com

Facebook: https://www.facebook.com/jcaddesigninc/

YouTube:
https://www.youtube.com/channel/UCNOetiapVHzg-kyF-_rIskg

LinkedIn: https://www.linkedin.com/in/jason-vander-griendt-j-cad-inc-5b97b53b/

Sketfab (Virtual Reality Design): https://sketchfab.com/jcad

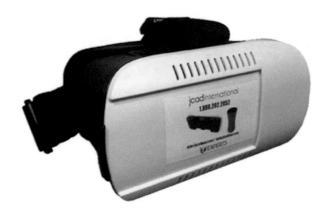

Ask us how we can design your project in virtual reality!

Contact Jason through http://jcadusa.com/contact/, on 1-888-202-2052 or at info@jcadusa.com for a free quote on your next product idea, for media requests, or if you just want to talk shop

Contact Jason through http://jcadusa.com/contact/, on 1-888-202-2052 or at info@jcadusa.com for a free quote on your next product idea, for media requests, or if you just want to talk shop

Made in the USA
Columbia, SC
07 January 2018